North Yorkshire

Keith Wadd

COUNTRYSIDE BOOKS
NEWBURY BERKSHIRE

First Published 2006
© Keith Wadd, 2006

COUNTRYSIDE BOOKS
3 Catherine Road
Newbury, Berkshire

To view our complete range of books,
please visit us at
www.countrysidebooks.co.uk

ISBN 1 85306 966 3
EAN 9 78185306 966 6

*For the Harrogate Rambling Club and the Harrogate Group
of the Ramblers' Association, with whom I have spent countless
happy hours exploring the paths of North Yorkshire*

Cover picture of Swaledale supplied by Derek Forss

Photographs by the author
Designed by Peter Davies, Nautilus Design
Produced through MRM Associates Ltd, Reading
Printed by Information Press Ltd, Oxford

Contents

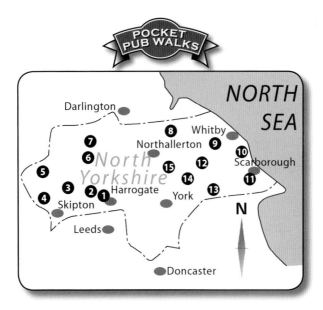

Area map showing location of the walks

Introduction

This book will act as your guide to walking in some of the best countryside in England. North Yorkshire contains the Yorkshire Dales and the North York Moors (both of which are National Parks) and many miles of attractive coastline. Outstanding areas of the Wolds are in North Yorkshire, and there is also the well-wooded, rolling landscape of the Howardian Hills.

These fifteen circular routes are ideal for a morning walk and a late lunch, or an afternoon walk followed by an evening meal. The featured pubs all serve hot food and they welcome walkers. Many of them are ancient hostelries full of character. Furthermore, they all serve real ale (that's the sort where the yeast hasn't been killed off).

The walks are good rambles in their own right. They wend their way over a variety of terrain, not just across moorland or meadow, but in woodland and by water, and through hamlets and villages. On every route you will find plenty of enjoyable views.

It is important to be properly equipped for your outing. Some of the walks can be done in trainers or strong shoes in the summer, but boots are a better bet, and they are a necessity for winter walking. The sunniest days can sometimes turn nasty, particularly in hill country, so it is a good idea to carry waterproofs in your rucksack as well as a drink and perhaps a snack. The sketch maps with each walk will guide you round the route but the appropriate Ordnance Survey Explorer or Outdoor Leisure map will also be useful.

Finally, please remember to seek prior permission if you wish to leave your car in the pub car park during the walk though several of the routes are accessible by public transport.

Happy walking in North Yorkshire!

Keith Wadd

Acknowledgement

I thank Anne, my wife, for her company on several of the walks and for lots of other support.

Publisher's Note

We hope that you obtain considerable enjoyment from this book; great care has been taken in its preparation. However, changes of landlord and actual closures are sadly not uncommon. Likewise, although at the time of publication all routes followed public rights of way or permitted paths, diversion orders can be made and permissions withdrawn.

We cannot, of course, be held responsible for such diversion orders and any inaccuracies in the text which result from these or any other changes to the routes nor any damage which might result from walkers trespassing on private property. We are anxious, though, that all details covering the walks and the pubs are kept up to date and would therefore welcome information from readers which would be relevant to future editions.

The simple sketch maps that accompany the walks in the book are based on notes made by the author whilst checking out the routes on the ground. For the benefit of a proper map, however, we do recommend that you purchase the relevant Ordnance Survey sheet covering your walk. The Ordnance Survey maps are widely available, especially through booksellers and local newsagents.

The Old Bell

I **chose this Harrogate route** to set the scene for a book of North Yorkshire pub walks because it is centrally placed and has extensive views that give a perspective on the whole county. You can look across the Vale of York to the North York Moors and the Wolds, and from a nearby viewpoint you can see the Pennines and the hills that enclose Nidderdale. The surprisingly well-wooded circuit is close to the town, but it is rarely near buildings. The walk can be combined with a visit to Harlow Carr Gardens, the northern showpiece of the Royal Horticultural Society.

Harrogate rose to prominence as a spa town in the 19th century, and it retains the fine buildings and spaciousness of its heyday. Today, it is a commuter town, conference venue, upmarket shopping centre and a good location for a holiday exploring Yorkshire. For a brief history of the town, visit the small museum in the Pump Room.

North Yorkshire

Distance – 5 miles.

OS Explorer 289 Leeds or 297 Lower Wharfedale and Washburn Valley. GR 297555.

Starting point The Old Bell, Harrogate.

How to get there The Old Bell is on Royal Parade, more or less opposite the Pump Room museum and close to the entrance to the Valley Gardens. There is no car park at the pub, and the best bet is to leave your car beyond the meter zone on or near Kent Road or Kent Avenue (see sketch map). There is a half hourly rail service from Leeds, an hourly one from York and an excellent bus service from Leeds and Ripon (No 67).

THE PUB The **Old Bell** was opened as recently as 1999. However, there was a pub on the site called the Bell prior to the building of Royal Parade. Part of the premises now occupied by the Old Bell was a saddler's for many years, and more recently a café and restaurant. The other part used to be Farrah's Harrogate Toffee Shop. The present establishment, however, was immediately popular and includes Bill Clinton amongst its visitors. Food on offer includes the Old Bell fish pie topped with potato and cheese, or the traditional Irish stew with home-made soda bread. The real ales are Black Sheep, Caledonian Deuchars, Rooster's and Taylor's, plus four guest beers. There is also a Connoisseurs' Beer Menu.

Open all day from 12 noon; bar food is available from 12 noon till 2.30 pm and 6 pm to 7 pm on Mondays to Saturdays, and the brasserie does food from 7 pm to 9.30 pm on Mondays to Thursdays and 6 pm to 10 pm on Friday and Saturday.
☎ *01423 507930*

1 Go through the gateway of the **Valley Gardens**, one of England's many fine public parks: what more grandiose a start to a walk than this? Walk straight up the gardens with the stream on the left. Continue beside **Bogs Field** (it doesn't matter which side). This has been described as 'a wonder of the natural world' and is where 36 mineral springs, each one unique, come to the surface. Climb gently past the tennis courts on the left. Keep on the main path as you approach the pine woods, and ignore the path signposted to **Harlow Carr**. Continue through the woods, cross a road and go up a broad tarmac road with fine ornamental hollies. Turn left between greenhouses, past a circular stone water tower on the left and a charming square stone tower on the right (now the premises of the **Astronomy Society**). An extensive view unfolds across the **Vale of York**. The **Cleveland escarpment** (the finest in the land) extends from beyond Osmotherley to the clearly visible **Kilburn White Horse** (see Walk 15). Further right you can see **York Minster** (in winter it's just to the right of the

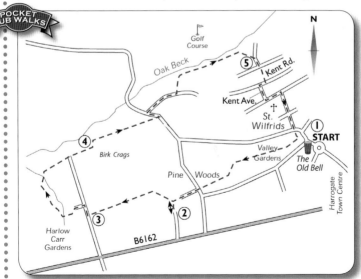

North Yorkshire

The Pump Room and entrance to the Valley Gardens.

plume of smoke from the sugar beet factory). Beyond are the **Yorkshire Wolds** (see Walk 13).

2 Retrace your steps to the greenhouses and go straight on through a gap beside a gate. Slant left across the wide grassy area to join a broad path into the pine woods. After a short distance, wide views appear on the right. The prominent low wooded hill on the right is **How Hill** close to **Fountains Abbey**; then further left are the hills enclosing **Nidderdale** backed by **Great Whernside** (2,308 ft); the broad rounded hill straight ahead is not surprisingly **Round Hill** (1,341 ft).

3 The path comes out on a tarmac road at **Harlow Carr Gardens**. If you want to include a visit (an attractive colourful experience whatever the time of year), turn left for the entrance. Otherwise, turn right for a few yards, then first left down to the **Harrogate Arms**. Go to the left of the pub, cross the bridge over the stream and then bear right along a wooded path close to a fence on the left. Shortly after a footbridge, turn right by a **Ringway Footpath** sign (the Harrogate Ringway, devised by the local

Ramblers' Association group, is a 20-mile circular walk round Harrogate) and descend steeply to cross two more footbridges. The attractive woodland path climbs to a gap in the fence, then bears right close to the fence. Go immediately to the right of substantial rocks and climb steeply to footpath signs. Bear left along the top of the rocks to **Birk Crag**, a splendid airy place.

4 Continue down a steep path, which bears right along a grassy terrace. Continue along a level path through attractive woodland to reach a road. Turn left down the road, then turn sharp right by the **Ringway Footpath** sign along a broad unsurfaced road. Shortly after it begins to climb, turn left between houses down the **Ringway Footpath**, which leads into woodland and down to the **Oak Beck** at the **Iron Bridge**, Harrogate's oldest bridge, reputedly used for carrying ironstone to nearby Kirby Overblow. Unfortunately, the bridge is fenced off. The path continues down the wooded valley with charming views of the beck on the left, then climbs up to a road.

5 Leave the **Ringway Footpath** and go up the road to the right, then up the path at the left of the house straight ahead. Turn right along **Kent Road**, then first left down **Kent Avenue** with the large bulk of **St Wilfrid's church** straight ahead. Turn left at the church, then turn right and along **Clarence Drive** to the **Valley Gardens**. The **Old Bell** is a few yards further on.

Place of interest nearby

Knaresborough, 4 miles away, is a much older town than Harrogate. Most of its castle, which is on a spectacular cliff-top site overlooking the River Nidd, failed to survive the Civil War, but an impressive keep still remains. There is an admission charge to the keep, but the rest of the site is a public park.
☎ 01423 556188.

2 Pateley Bridge

The Royal Oak

This is one of the best half-day walks I know. There is an attractive stretch by the River Nidd, a lake and a tarn, extensive woodland, an exhilarating gritstone edge, and many splendid views, both into Nidderdale and beyond. The Nidd surfaces on the eastern slopes of Great Whernside. In the top end of the valley are the large Angram and Scar House reservoirs built to supply water to Bradford, and a massive civil engineering project in their time. The sides of the valley around Pateley Bridge are well wooded and full of craggy outcrops, the most spectacular at Brimham Rocks to the east. Nidderdale used to be a hive of industry; there was extensive lead mining on the slopes of Greenhow Hill, quarrying was widepread and there was a substantial linen industry.

Distance – 6 miles.

OS Explorer 298 Nidderdale. GR 158655.

Starting point The Riverside car park at Pateley Bridge.

How to get there *Leave the A61 at Ripley and take the B6165/B6265 to Pateley Bridge. Turn left at the bottom of the High Street and continue for ¼ mile to where the road ends at the Riverside car park. At the time of writing, all-day parking was £1. There is an hourly Harrogate to Pateley Bridge bus service.*

THE PUB The **Royal Oak** is a pleasant and popular small pub with interesting local photographs and a good fire in winter. There is a beer garden across the road at the front of the pub and, in warm weather, a meal or a drink can be enjoyed with pleasant Nidderdale views. The large food menu includes a 'Sunday' roast every day and an excellent 8 oz sirloin steak, and other dishes are listed on a specials board. The real ales are Banks's, Marston's Pedigree and John Smith's.

Food is available from 12 noon till 9 pm every day.
Telephone: 01423 711577

1. Drop down to the hardcore path beside the river, turn left and follow it downstream. It is attractive walking along the tree-lined banks of the swift-flowing river. After ½ mile the path swings right near a weir and broadens into a lane, with an extensive lake on one side and a former mill leat at the other.

2. Turn right at the T-junction at the bottom of **Glasshouses** and take the metalled road over the bridge. Go left at the fork

North Yorkshire

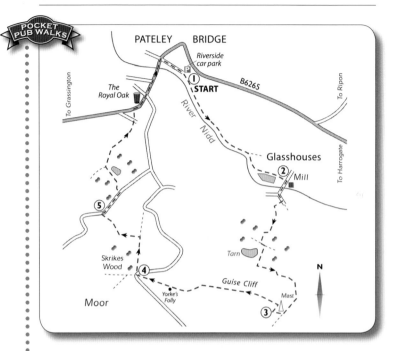

POCKET PUB WALKS

PATELEY BRIDGE

Riverside car park

START

B6265

To Grassington

The Royal Oak

River Nidd

To Ripon

To Harrogate

Glasshouses

② *Mill*

⑤

Skrikes Wood

④

Tarn

Guise Cliff

Moor

Yorke's Folly

Mast

③

N

immediately afterwards. The finely proportioned stone building on the left just beyond the river is the former **Glasshouses Mill**. After a few yards, the road forks again by some cottages; take the right turn along a lane up the hillside. After some houses, the lane becomes a footpath and leads into **Parker Wood** by a stile at the top of some stone steps. Go immediately right for a few yards and then continue up the hillside in attractive woodland. The path twists and turns but is never far away from a decrepit wire fence on the right. Turn left at the T-junction of paths, then shortly afterwards turn right and continue on a rocky path which climbs quite steeply. **Guisecliff Tarn** is close-by on the right. Shortly after the tarn, the path swings left and descends slightly then takes a fairly level course through the wood, passing on the left a large rock suitable for climbing practice. At the end of the wood the path climbs steeply up the hillside to a large mast. This is a good viewpoint and there are extensive views eastwards across the **Vale of York** to **Sutton Bank** and the **Wolds**.

3 Turn right along the fence round the back of the mast, then go along a well-trodden path on the top of **Guise Cliff**. It is a splendid, airy walk along the gritstone edge with good views into **Nidderdale**, and the notice about 'dangerous crevasses' should not be taken lightly as there are some fearsome holes in the ground close to the path. After a stile the path follows a wall on the right, and there are views of **Greenhow Hill** ahead. Immediately after a ladder stile, the path goes beside the bizarrely-shaped **Yorke's Folly**, named after John Yorke. The Yorkes were a powerful local family and the folly was erected around 1800 to provide work at a time of local unemployment. Follow the rocky path down to the nearby road.

Yorke's Folly near Guise Cliff.

[4] Go through a kissing gate at the other side of the road, and follow the path down the hillside. There are fine views of **Nidderdale** with **Pateley Bridge** coming into view. Go over the ladder stile and into **Skrikes Wood**. Ignore the stile at the bottom of the wood, and keep inside the wood with the wall on the right. The clear path descends through further woodland, and crosses **Fosse Gill** by a substantial footbridge to reach a road.

[5] Turn right along the road and, after 300 yards or so, turn left through a gateway marked '**Moor View Kennels**. Immediately after the gateway turn right on a path into **Fishpond Wood**. The path goes to the left of a pond, crosses a rudimentary footbridge and enters a field. Turn right along the wall and there, some fine old stone steps will help you up the steep bank. Continue in the same direction down the next field with good views of **Pateley Bridge** ahead. Turn left along the road and immediately after a stream is crossed go over a low stile on the right. Make for the far corner of the field and go over a stile just before a gate. Turn right down the B6265 (take care, it's quite busy) and the **Royal Oak** is just round the corner. Continue into Pateley Bridge from the Royal Oak, then immediately after the bridge over the river, turn right on to **Nidd Walk**. The impressive stone building on the left with the stepped gables is the former **railway station**. **Riverside car park** is a short distance further on.

Places of interest nearby

Brimham Rocks are a remarkable outcrop of gritstone rocks weathered into extraordinary shapes. There are several acres of rocks on a well-wooded site owned by the National Trust. The rocks are five miles from Pateley Bridge, and most easily reached via the B6265 road to Ripon.
☎ 01423 780688

The Racehorses Hotel

This is an outstanding walk in the magnificent limestone landscape of Upper Wharfedale and Littondale. The views are stunning. There are steep-sided, wooded hillsides, craggy limestone outcrops and a mosaic of walled pastures. Rarely can the works of man have blended so well with nature (albeit accidentally), and the whole landscape is a visual delight. No wonder so many people love the Yorkshire Dales and fiercely protect them. You should be prepared for two long climbs on this route but, apart from short stretches, they are not really steep. There are also some rocky bits where caution is necessary, particularly when the rocks are wet.

Kettlewell at some time in its past has had a market and a cotton mill and has been a lead-mining settlement. Now it is an attractive village almost entirely given over to tourism.

North Yorkshire

The **Racehorses Hotel** is on the left by the hump-back bridge in the middle of the village and dates back to 1740. It is as attractive inside as out, with a large stone fireplace (with a welcoming fire in winter), stone floors and a carved wooden bar. Real ales served here include Black Sheep and Timothy Taylor, and the beer that I drank as soon as I got into the pub was perfect. Steak and ale pie is among the choice of food on the lunch menu, and daily specials such as lamb hot pot are listed on a board. There is a separate dinner menu in the evening. The Racehorses is residential with en suite rooms.

Food is available from 12 noon till 2 pm (3 pm on Saturday and Sunday) and from 6.30 pm to 9 pm.
☎ *01756 760233*

1 Leave **Kettlewell** by the main road down the valley towards **Grassington**, cross the bridge over the **Wharfe** and continue along the road for nearly ¼ mile to the footpath sign (**FP Hawkswick 2 miles**) by a gate on the right. The path climbs the hillside through attractive woodland with plenty of hazels. After a gate, keep to the wall on the right, then go through a gap in a

Distance – 6 miles.

OS Explorer Outdoor Leisure 30 Yorkshire Dales: Northern and Central areas. GR 969723.

Starting point The Racehorses Hotel, Kettlewell.

How to get there *Kettlewell is in Upper Wharfedale. From Skipton take the B6265 to Threshfield, near Grassington, then the B6160 past the spectacular Kilnsey Crag to Kettlewell. There is a two-hourly bus service from Skipton.*

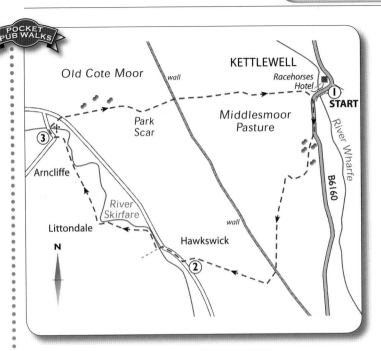

KETTLEWELL

Racehorses Hotel

START

Old Cote Moor

wall

Middlesmoor Pasture

Park Scar

River Wharfe

B6160

3

Arncliffe

River Skirfare

Littondale

N

wall

Hawkswick

2

wall. Climb steeply beside woodland for a short distance (this is **Gate Cote Scar**), and the path then turns right to a ladder stile beside a broken wall. The path swings left to another ladder stile, then continues to climb as it passes two cairns. It then levels out on upland pasture, which is delightful easy walking. At the next stile **Littondale** comes into view, and after a few yards you can look left down **Wharfedale** and see **Kilnsey Crag**. The path swings right and continues down the hillside close to a wall on the left. It is enjoyable walking: grassy underfoot and fine views up **Littondale**. The path comes into a walled lane, which soon drops into **Hawkswick**.

2 Turn right and walk along the road through the village. Shortly after leaving the village, turn left across the footbridge over the

River Skirfare, then turn right immediately afterwards on the footpath signposted to **Arncliffe**. The path keeps close to the bank of the river at first, then crosses meadows before rejoining the river. In spring and summer you may see sand martins (they have brown wings). There are fine views of both sides of the dale: limestone crags on the left and wooded slopes on the right. Go to the right of a stone barn, through a gate, to the left of a clump of trees, then veer right to rejoin the riverbank. The path goes to the right of a walled garden and to the left of **Arncliffe churchyard**. From the lychgate, there is an attractive view of the church, which has a Perpendicular (mid-14th to mid-16th century) tower, and the churchyard has fine yews.

3 Turn right when the road is reached, then take the footpath signposted to **Kettlewell** immediately after the bridge. Cross another road, then let climbing commence! Take the clear path that slants up the hillside to a stone step stile, then continue in the same direction up the wooded slope. Keep glancing back for outstanding views over **Arncliffe** with the deep valley of **Cowside Beck** particularly prominent. The path becomes rocky as it climbs the wooded **Park Scar** but there is no serious difficulty. Carry on in the same direction towards the top of a wall when the path enters a field, and cross a ladder stile. The clear path climbs gently through heather moorland (a surprise after the limestone!) and it swings left after the second signpost. Continue to glance back for views. When the ridge of **Old Cote Moor** is reached at a ladder stile, there are stunning views of **Wharfedale** ahead. Continue in the same direction as you descend into **Kettlewell** with views of **Great Whernside** straight ahead and **Buckden Pike** on the left. Don't go through the gate, but cross the wall by a ladder stile lower down. Further on, a rocky limestone cleft provides an interesting challenge (but the timorous can avoid it by adding a few hundred yards), and the path soon leads down to the bridge over the **Wharfe** in **Kettlewell village**.

A fine view towards Littondale.

Places of interest nearby

Grassington, 7 miles down the valley, is an engaging small town, the houses in the centre grouped round an attractive small square. In the town is the Upper Wharfedale Museum, and the Yorkshire Dales National Park Centre (close to the car park) is also well worth visiting.

4 **Giggleswick**

The Harts Head Hotel

This is a limestone walk on paths of springy turf that are a delight to tread. Giggleswick Scar, a low limestone cliff with several caves, is a particular feature of the circuit, and it also borders the great Craven Fault, which is of considerable interest to geologists. All of the 'Three Peaks' can be seen along the way. In spring and summer the song of the skylark, the cry of the curlew and the churr of the wheatear can be heard, and orchids should be easy to find. As limestone drains so well, there are very few wet patches, and the route is an excellent choice for a bright winter day.

Settle, visited on the longer walk, is a town of character whose market gained its charter in 1249. The limestone houses in the centre date back to the 17th and 18th centuries and above them is a wooded crag, usually with a flag on it. The town is now famed as the starting point of the Settle–Carlisle railway line, and a journey on this scenic high-level route across the Pennines is strongly recommended.

THE PUB There is a very welcoming atmosphere at the **Harts Head Hotel**, a former coaching inn that dates back to the 1700s, and it still offers overnight accommodation. Attractive, freshly-prepared meals such as seafood crêpe or chicken and bacon melt are served. The real ales include Copper Dragon, Black Sheep and Tetley's, as well as beers from the local Litton and Wharfedale breweries. There is an attractive south-facing beer garden.

Food is available from 12 noon till 2.30 pm and from 5.30 pm to 9 pm.
☎ *01729 822086*

Distance – 6 or 7½ miles.

OS Explorer Outdoor Leisure 41 Forest of Bowland and Ribbblesdale. GR 813641.

Starting point The Harts Head Hotel, Giggleswick.

How to get there *Giggleswick is 17 miles from Skipton. Follow the A65 Skipton–Kendall road and turn off northwards on the B6480. Continue along the B6480 through Settle to Giggleswick, and the Harts Head is on the left. Park on the B6480 or in the centre of the village (see map for best place). Giggleswick is easily reachable by train, but note that Settle Station is more conveniently placed for this walk than Giggleswick Station, and you would join the route at the railway bridge in point 6.*

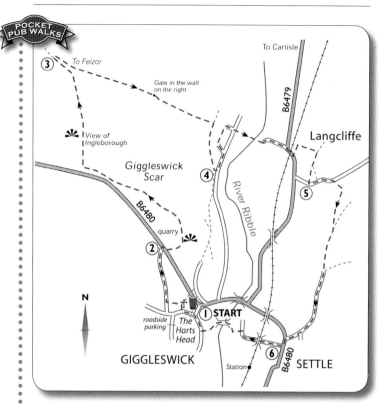

To Carlisle

To Feizor

③

Gate in the wall
on the right

B6479

View of
Ingleborough

Langcliffe

Giggleswick
Scar

④

River Ribble

⑤

B6480

quarry

②

N

St Alkelda's

roadside
parking

The
Harts
Head

① START

⑥

B6480

GIGGLESWICK

Station

SETTLE

1 Turn right after leaving the **Harts Head**, and down the lane into **Giggleswick**. Turn right at the bottom, then go through the lychgate into the churchyard of **St Alkelda's**, a pleasant limestone building, much of it 15th century. Turn right after the churchyard and go along a lane, then turn left through a stone gap stile immediately after the last house. Walk through the grounds of **Giggleswick School** to reach a tarmac road. Turn right and follow the road for about ⅓ mile to the B6480. Cross the road to a low stile immediately to the right of the 'Giggleswick Quarry' sign.

2 The path goes steeply up the hillside by the boundary fence of the quarry and furnishes interesting views of what happens inside. Keep close to the quarry fence when the top of the hill is reached, where are fine views of **Pen-y-ghent**. There is also a good view of **Pendle Hill**. At the end of the quarry, slant left to a marker post. A clear grassy path onto **Giggleswick Scar** can then be picked up. It follows an attractive, undulating terrace just below the scar, and diversions can be made to caves on the right. There are views of the **Forest of Bowland moors** on the left. At the end of the scar the path swings right to a gated stile, then, after a brief steep climb up a field, a fine view of **Ingleborough** rears up ahead. Beyond it, just to the right, there is a snatch of **Whernside**. After about ½ mile from when the view of Ingleborough first appeared, go through a gate (or over a ladder stile) at the end of a long field, then briefly continue along a wall on the left to a signpost.

3 Turn sharp right and go up the grassy hillside. The line is to the left of a lone tree, which soon comes into view on the horizon. Go over a ladder stile by the gate, and continue in the same direction in the next field and through two more gates. A few yards after the last gate, go through a gate in the wall on the right, then keep in the same direction with the wall on the left. The hill straight ahead is **Warrendale Knotts**. Keep in the same direction after the next gate, and descend a rocky field to the right-hand gap of two gaps in the wall. Cross the next field to the left-hand ladder stile of the two available, then descend to a signpost. Turn right and follow the path alongside a wall to **Stackhouse Lane**.

4 *For the shorter walk,* keep on the path in the field close to the wall alongside **Stackhouse Lane**. The path goes over an access road, crosses a field to a stile, then keeps in a field to the left of a wood. It then enters a tree-lined lane (don't go down the lane on the left). When the lane becomes a residential road, go down the path on the right between **Pendle View** and **Pathways**.

The lane into Settle.

Cross the B6480 to a walled path through the graveyards to **Giggleswick** and retrace your steps to the pub.

For the longer walk, turn left along **Stackhouse Lane**, then soon turn left on a lane by a large beech tree. Take the first turn right, then turn right at the next junction. Go straight across **Stackhouse Lane**, and along a walled path to the **River Ribble** (which unlike other Yorkshire rivers flows into the Irish Sea). Go over the footbridge and up the lane straight ahead. Briefly turn right and onto the B6479 as it crosses the famous **Settle–Carlisle railway line**, then turn left along an unsurfaced lane and over a stile on the right. Go to the top of the field, then turn right and along a walled lane into Langcliffe.

5 Turn left on the road up the hill past the primary school (but first admire the charming village green). Go through a gate to the right of the road and climb steeply up the side of a field. The path then bends right and takes a level course close to a wall on the right across several fields, with fine views down into the valley. The path leads into a walled lane and descends into the attractive small town of **Settle**.

6 Cross the main street and take the lane signposted '**Friends Meeting House**' (also 'toilets'). On the skyline, the dome with the prominent nipple is the chapel of **Giggleswick School**. Continue under the railway bridge and past **Booths**. Just before the fire station turn left, then right at the road junction, and round a converted mill. Cross the **Ribble** by the footbridge, then slant left along a walled path to **Bankwell Street**. Turn right and in a few yards you are in the middle of **Giggleswick** from where you can retrace your steps to the **Harts Head**.

Places of interest nearby

The famous **Settle and Carlisle line**, opened in 1875, was built by the Midland Railway to avoid using the tracks of a rival company. It is probably the most scenic railway in England and has a magnificent route across the head of Ribblesdale, Dentdale, Garsdale and Wensleydale before dropping into the Eden valley. Visit www.settle-carlisle. co.uk for further details.

5 **Ribblehead**

The Station Inn

Whernside at **2,416 ft above sea level** is Yorkshire's highest peak. It can be climbed by a good circular walk from Ribblehead, which is itself 1,000 ft above sea level, so some of the hard work has already been done! The route of the ascent is easy, on a broad firm path, with scarcely a steep gradient the whole way. Take extra layers of clothing, as it is usually a different climate on top, and often blowing a gale. If the forecast isn't good, and especially after a period of heavy rain, leave the walk for another day – a good principle is: 'If you can't see it, don't do it.' But in decent weather, the walk up Whernside is a grand Pennine experience. The view from the top is outstanding and includes the sea (Morecambe Bay) and the Lake District.

Distance – 7½ miles.

OS Explorer Outdoor Leisure 2 Yorkshire Dales: Southern and Western areas. GR 763791.

Starting point The Station Inn, Ribblehead.

How to get there *From Settle take the B6479 up the Ribble valley to Ribblehead, then at the T-junction turn left along the B6255 to the Station Inn. There is parking close to the road junction. Or take the train to Ribblehead station.*

Whernside has only recently become Yorkshire's highest peak. That honour used to be held by Mickle Fell at 2,591 ft till it went on a free transfer to County Durham. Whernside is to be distinguished from Great Whernside near Kettlewell, which despite its title is less great and can only manage a mere 2,308 ft above sea level.

THE PUB

The **Station Inn**, close to Ribblehead station, is deservedly popular with walkers and railway buffs. From the 'Loo With a View' there is a stunning view of Whernside. The menu includes a wide range of dishes, and there are also daily specials. You can have giant Yorkshire puds with a choice of fillings, or try the Cumberland Feast (Cumberland sausages with seasonal vegetables, wholegrain mustard mash and onion gravy). The real ales are from Skipton Brewery, Black Sheep, Jennings and Theakston. The Station Inn does bed and breakfast and there is also a bunk house.

Food is available from 12.30 pm to 2.30 pm and 6.30 pm (6 pm on Saturdays) to 8.30 pm.
☎ *01524 241274*

North Yorkshire

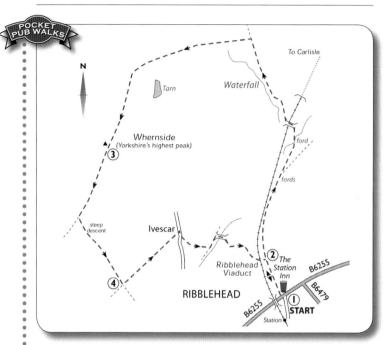

POCKET
PUB WALKS

To Carlisle

Waterfall

N

Tarn

Whernside
(Yorkshire's highest peak)
(3)

ford

fords

steep
descent

Ivescar

(4)

Ribblehead
Viaduct

(2) The
Station
Inn

B6255

B6479

RIBBLEHEAD

B6255

**(1)
START**

Station

1 Go over the ladder stile at the back of the **Station Inn car park** and slant right to pick up the broad track to the **Ribblehead Viaduct** with the whaleback shape of Whernside straight ahead. The viaduct is a fine construction of 24 arches built of local limestone, and is the most impressive architectural feature on the Settle–Carlisle line. Near the foot of the viaduct is the site of the construction camp for the railway workers. It housed over 2,000 people and had a school and library. It is now a scheduled monument, though there are precious few remains. It must have been an inhospitable place to live, and work on the railway was hard and dangerous. Many of the workers died; their unmarked graves are in the churchyard at nearby **Chapel le Dale**. Also at the foot of the bridge are many shakeholes, hollows where the acid water of the moors has bitten into the limestone.

2 Take the crushed-stone path that goes to the right of the viaduct, and keep the railway on the left. Look back for a fine view of **Pen-y-Ghent**, the shapely hill further down the **Ribblesdale valley**. There are small streams to ford, and they become more challenging after wet weather. Bear left when the tracks divide, and cross the larger ford over **Little Dale Beck**, but take no chances if the stream is in spate and, regrettably, there is no alternative route. Cross the **Settle–Carlisle line** and note the aqueduct on the left beside the bridge, and the entrance to **Bleamoor Tunnel** on the right. The path now climbs steadily to the right of **Force Gill**, which has an impressive waterfall. Turn left over the stile by the signpost to **Whernside**, and continue ascending. There is an unnamed tarn on the left and peat hags all around. The path swings left and eventually reaches the Whernside ridge. As you walk along the ridge to the summit, nip up to the wall on the right for views down into **Dentdale**.

3 The summit is not a discrete peak but is recognisable by a trig point over the wall beyond the shelter. The view is outstanding. The majestic table-top peak of **Ingleborough** dominates the prospect straight ahead to the south, with **Pendle Hill** beyond. Further to the right is **Morecambe Bay**, and further round to the west are the mountains of the **Lake District**. In the foreground are the **Howgill Fells**. Some miles away to the east are **Great Whernside** and **Buckden Pike**, and beyond them is **Pen Hill**. Below in the valley is the **Ribblehead Viaduct**, and the railway can be traced for several

Ribblehead Viaduct and Whernside.

miles north after it emerges from **Bleamoor Tunnel**. After appreciating the view, keep going along the ridge, which falls in a series of gigantic steps. After the last one, follow the main path left, which drops steeply into the valley. It is advisable to watch where you're putting your feet on this stretch, and ignore the view for a while.

4 When the path leads into a lane by a stone barn on the left, turn left on a path signposted to **Winterscales**. The path goes just to the right of the farm, and continues in the same direction through fields just below the rocks of a limestone scar. There is a good view of **Whernside** to the left, and the **Ribblehead Viaduct** dominates the view straight ahead. The path joins a farm road, which leads to the farm buildings at **Ivescar**. Turn sharp right towards the end of the farmyard, then go over a step stile on the left immediately after a barn. Walk diagonally across the field to a step stile and continue up a small hill and down the other side, keeping the wall on your left. Go over the stile in the left corner of the next field, then cross the following field to a ladder stile just beyond the right-hand pylon. Turn left along the road, then immediately after the gate turn right and cross the stream (the continuation of **Little Dale Beck** encountered earlier in the walk). Keep the farm buildings on the left and walk along the farm access road, which goes under the massive stone arches of the **Ribblehead Viaduct**. Now retrace your steps to the **Station Inn**.

Places of interest nearby

On the road to nearby Ingleton are the **White Scar Caves**. Telephone: 01524 241244.

Ingleton is at the junction of the rivers Doe and Twiss, and both have impressive waterfalls. The falls can be visited on an attractive circular walk.

6 West Burton

The Fox and Hounds

West Burton is a pretty village of stone houses, which have grown up on either side of its green. It has kept its primary school, and also still has a butcher's, post office and village store. And, of course, the pub. This is a walk in scenery as beautiful as you will find anywhere. Although it is a short-ish circuit, it climbs a fair way up the hillside and is quite steep in places – and the descent is very steep. The hillsides in Wensleydale and other valleys in the Yorkshire Dales tend to rise in a series of giant steps, the precipitous parts of which are called scars, and these often extend along the valley sides for a mile or more. This walk slants up one of these scars, Morpeth Scar, then turns along the top of it on an enjoyable green lane. A succession of outstanding views into Wensleydale and Bishopdale provide a special feature of the walk. There is also woodland, a

North Yorkshire

Distance – 3 or 4 miles.

OS Explorer Outdoor Leisure 30 Yorkshire Dales: Northern and Central areas. GR 017867.

Starting point The Fox and Hounds, West Burton.

How to get there Take the A684 along Wensleydale to Hawes, and 6 miles west of Leyburn turn off southwards along the B6160. After almost 2 miles turn left into West Burton village. The Fox and Hounds is at the top end of the village green, on the right. Park on the road close to the pub.

fine waterfall, and an opportunity to examine the rocks of the scar at close quarters. The longer route takes you into pleasant meadows in the lower part of the Walden valley.

THE PUB The **Fox and Hounds** is a small and pleasant village pub that dates back to the 18th century. It is popular with visitors and, in the summer you can sit outside and enjoy the delightful view over the village green. It offers a good range of main courses and specials, including steak and kidney pie, venison casserole and curry. The real ales are Black Sheep, Copper Dragon, John Smith's and Tetley's. Overnight accommodation is available.

Food is served from 12 noon to 2 pm (2.30 pm on Sundays) and from 6 pm to 8.30 pm.
Telephone: 01969 663111

1 Go down to the bottom right-hand corner of the green, and just after the shop called **Moorland Cats** where the road swings left, turn down a lane on the right, which almost immediately leads to an attractive open area by the **Walden Beck**. There is an

impressive waterfall 100 yards upstream, and attractive wooded slopes. Cross the stream by the bridge and bear left up to a gated stile. Follow the path up the field to the right of a stone barn and continue in the same direction to a stile into a wood.

2 Turn left, signposted '**Morpeth Gate**' along an attractive woodland path. Turn right when a lane (**Morpeth Gate**) is reached and follow it up the hillside. Although it is stony, it is tree-lined and pleasant, and there are increasingly good views to the left into **Wensleydale**. At one point, **Bolton Castle** can be seen. Near the top on the right is the rock face of **Morpeth Scar**.

3 Turn right at a footpath sign pointing to '**West Burton via Hudson Quarry Lane**'. The view is particularly fine at this point. There are views up **Bishopdale** to the left, as well as into **Wensleydale**. The table-top hill ahead is **Addlebrough**. Continue along the path to **Hudson Quarry Lane**, which soon becomes an enjoyable walled green lane. **Dove Scar** is on the left. The lane leaves its walls, and goes across the top of two fields to reach a signpost. The valley straight ahead is the **Walden Beck valley**, and the hill at the top of it is **Buckden Pike** (2,302 ft). Almost at your feet in the valley below is **West Burton**.

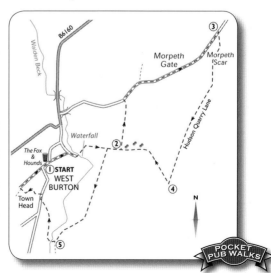

4 Now turn right and follow the steep path down the hillside. Make for a post, and then a gate stile. The views continue to be a delight. The path zigzags down **Morpeth Scar** to a gap in the wall, and then to a stile by an ash tree. The path continues to descend steeply through woodland to reach the **Morpeth Gate signpost** at point 2, which was passed earlier in the walk. Retrace your steps down the field to a signpost at the corner of a wall.

For the shorter walk, carry straight on and retrace your steps into **West Burton**.

For the longer walk, turn left on the path signposted '**Rockwith Bridge, Cote Bridge**'. It is a pleasant, clear route across several meadows. After a house called **Riddings** is passed on the right, the path drops gently (note the yellow-topped posts if there is doubt) and there are good views up the valley ahead.

5 Cross the **Walden Beck** on a substantial footbridge, and then the path slants up the hillside to the right to reach a road. Turn right briefly, then turn left along a lane signposted '**FP Town Head 200 Yds**'. Turn right when the lane reaches the farm at **Town Head**, and walk down the road into **West Burton**.

Places of interest nearby

Two miles away at **Aysgarth** are the famous **Aysgarth Falls**, one of the most visited places in the Pennines. There is the Top Force, Middle Force, and Lower Force with well signposted walks from which the falls can be viewed. There is also a good view of the Top Force from the road. **Aysgarth church**, close to the falls, has a fine rood screen and claims to have the largest churchyard in the country.

7 **Reeth**

The Black Bull Hotel

This walk is an introduction to Swaledale, one of the most wild and beautiful valleys in the Pennines. The first part of the circuit is in the tributary valley of Arkengarthdale and runs close to the foot of Fremington Edge, the high edge of grey limestone that dominates the view from outside the Black Bull. The route then goes over heather moorland to cross a low ridge that comes down from Calver Hill. Those who enjoy limestone walls and lots of them – also a variety of stiles – will appreciate the latter part of the walk. Swaledale once had a thriving lead industry with sites scattered over many parts of the valley. Remains of the industry can be seen at the end of Fremington Edge. Reeth, which is built round an extensive green, is the largest village in Swaledale and a major port of call on the popular Coast to Coast Walk. Its small museum is well worth a visit.

North Yorkshire

The **Black Bull Hotel**, which is Reeth's oldest pub and dates from 1680, is on the attractive village green. It has great character, with low beams and many an odd nook, and is popular with locals and visitors alike. In winter, its log fire will be much appreciated. Try the home-made pie of the day, or the trout with almonds, Real ales are Black Sheep, John Smith's and Theakston's (including Old Peculier). The Black Bull is residential.

Food is available every day from 12 noon till 2.30 pm and from 6 pm to 9.30 pm, but you will need to book in advance for the Sunday Carvery.
☎ *01748 884213*

1 Leave **Reeth** by the road to **Richmond** (B6270). Just after the end of the green turn left up the road to the museum, then go right almost immediately along a gap between houses (no signpost) which soon leads to a narrow walled path dropping steeply down to the valley. Turn right at the bottom on a path beside the **Arkle Beck**. Follow the path under the attractive stone road bridge, then turn right and go across the bridge.

Distance – 4 miles.

OS Explorer Outdoor Leisure 30 Yorkshire Dales: Northern and Central areas. GR 038993.

Starting point The Black Bull Hotel at Reeth.

How to get there Reeth is right in the middle of Swaledale, 10 miles from Richmond. Take the A6108 Richmond to Leyburn road, and 5 miles south-west of Richmond turn off westwards on the B6270 to Reeth. There is a parking on the village green (honesty box).

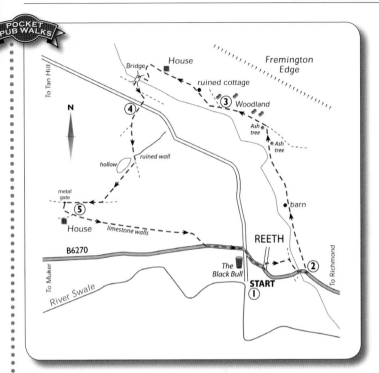

POCKET PUB WALKS

To Tan Hill

Bridge
House
Fremington Edge
ruined cottage
3 Woodland
Ash tree
Ash tree
4
N
hollow
ruined wall
metal gate
5
House
limestone walls
barn
REETH
B6270
To Muker
River Swale
The Black Bull
START
1
2
To Richmond

2 Go through a gated stile on the left immediately after the bridge, then left along a farm track close to the wall. There are already good views of **Fremington Edge**. Go through a gate and to the right of a stone barn, then keep close to the wall on the right. Cross a gated stile, then keep left and through a wide gap in the wall, and continue through the field to a farm gate. Do not descend on the farm track (not a right of way), but walk along a green terrace just to the left of an ash tree, and cross a ruined wall by the next ash tree (a fine large one) to join a well-used track. Go left and continue up the valley. The path leads into woodland (primroses in spring) and then to a footpath signpost close the **Arkle Beck**.

North Yorkshire

The stone barn and Fremington Edge near Reeth.

3 Take the footpath beside the stream (not the bridleway). After a gap in the wall, climb gently by the wall on the right past a ruined cottage. The path leads to a stile at the top of a steep bank, and here you are in splendid scenery close to the foot of **Fremington Edge**; the former lead workings are at the left end of the edge. Go straight to the house ahead and through the garden, then continue in the same direction in the field beyond, along a track which swings left and winds down to the river. Cross the bridge, and follow the track as it climbs the hillside to a road.

4 Go straight across the road* and onto the moorland part of the walk (open access land, but the route is on a right-of-way). Take the faint path up the hillside towards some prominent marsh grass. Where the path divides, take the left-hand option, and keep going in the same direction when it peters out. On the nearby skyline on the left is an untidy moustache of ruined wall and marsh grass, and you make for almost the top end of this where you will find a crushed-stone track. (* If you do not fancy this, go left along the road for about 300 hundred yards, then sharp right along the crushed-stone track to join the direct route). Go along the crushed-stone track past the ruined wall for a few yards, then turn right and walk along the left-hand side of an extensive hollow. When you get to the ridge, there is a magnificent view of **Swaledale**. Keep in the same direction and soon you will come to a track with a wall on the left. Keep along the track when the wall finishes, and then go through a metal gate and down a crushed-stone track.

5 Turn left off the track before you reach the house and go through a gap stile just to the left of the field corner, then follow a wall on the right. This is the limestone wall part of the walk, lots of walls enclosing lots of small fields. The general strategy is to keep going in the same direction. There are gap stiles, step stiles, gated stiles and various combinations – quite an interesting variety. Where the route becomes uncertain after a few fields, there is a concealed stile well to the left of the left-hand tree. In the penultimate field before the school (the large stone building with the diminutive spire), go a shade left to a wooden step stile close to the end of a wall. Now cross the field to a gate in the bottom corner, and turn left along the road past the school and back into **Reeth**.

Places of interest nearby

The **folk museum** at **Reeth** contains many items of interest from Swaledale's former lead mining industry. ☎ 01748 884118.

8 **Great Ayton**

The Royal Oak Hotel

The centre of Great Ayton is attractively sited beside the infant River Leven. Captain Cook spent his early years here, and there is the Captain Cook Schoolroom Museum and a youthful statue of him nearby. This walk takes you up to Roseberry Topping (1,051 ft), which looks like a miniature Matterhorn and is one of the most shapely peaks in Britain, courtesy of being sharpened up by landslides caused by mining and quarrying. It's an enjoyable climb, though steep in places, and the views are excellent. The shorter route goes to the top of Roseberry Topping and returns by a different route. The longer walk continues to Captain Cook's Monument on Easby Moor (1,064 ft), another fine viewpoint.

Distance – 4 or 7 miles.

OS Explorer Outdoor Leisure 26 North York Moors: Western area. GR 563107.

Starting point The Royal Oak Hotel on the High Street at Great Ayton.

How to get there Great Ayton is on the A173 Stokesley to Guisborough road. Immediately after the bridge over the river, turn right onto the High Street, and the Royal Oak is a third of a mile on the left. Park on the High Street near to the pub. Great Ayton has a station on the sparsely used Middlesbrough to Whitby line.

THE PUB

The **Royal Oak** is a family run residential hotel that dates back to the 18th century and still retains the beamed ceilings of the period. Winter visitors will appreciate its log fires. There is an extensive selection of bar food – for example, try the crayfish tail and asparagus salad on the lunch menu, or the pan-fried local black pudding on the evening menu. The real ales are Theakston Bitter, Old Peculier and Courage Directors.

Food is available nearly all day, from 9.30 am to 9.30 pm.
☎ *01642 722361*

[1] Turn left after leaving the **Royal Oak**, then left along **Newton Road** at the road junction. After a short distance, go along the public footpath on the right. The clear path keeps to the left side of fields as it gently climbs the hillside. There are views of **Easby Moor** and **Captain Cook's Monument**. The path keeps to the fence on the left in the field after the level crossing (good views

of the **Cleveland Hills**), then turns left into the woodland of **Cliff Ridge Wood**, which is owned by the National Trust. Much of the woodland covers the former **Cliff Rigg Quarry**, from which whinstone was extracted, an igneous rock that also underlies some of the course of Hadrian's Wall.

2 Keep straight on at the junction of paths and climb steeply up the wooded hillside. Turn left at the signpost at the top of the wood with the sharp peak of **Roseberry Topping** now in view. Turn right immediately after the next stile and keep close to the fence on the right. Go to the left of the house ahead and continue in the same direction, keeping the hedge on the right. **Roseberry Topping** is straight ahead and looks magnificent.

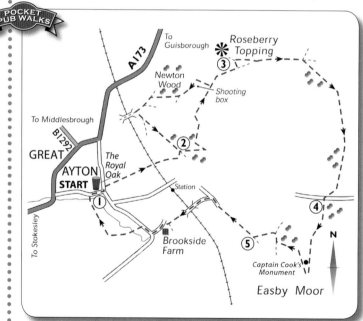

Just go straight for it on the clear path by the fence, but make a small detour to look at the unusual small stone building on the left, a restored 18th-century shooting box. Don't make a direct assault on the final peak, but keep to the path by the fence until it turns left opposite a gate, then winds its way to the top. The view is splendid: the **North York Moors** and the **Cleveland Hills**, up the **Tees plain** to the **Pennines**, over **Middlesbrough**, and the sea and lots of it!

3 *For the shorter walk*, retrace your steps off the summit, then go down the gully just to the right of the shooting box. Turn left after the gate into **Newton Wood** and follow the clear path at the top of the wood. Fork right when the path divides and slant down the hillside. Turn left at the bottom and follow the path close to the bottom of the wood. Turn sharp left where the woodland ends, 300 yards after the **National Trust sign**. Go past the quarry entrance, ignore the track that goes off to the right and keep straight on along the path that slants up the hillside. This soon levels out and becomes an attractive woodland path, which after ½ mile comes out at point 2, from where you return to **Great Ayton**.

For the longer walk, turn right at the summit then descend to the low ridge linking **Roseberry Topping** to the nearby moors. Keep by the fence/wall on the right and ascend the hillside to the left of a conifer wood. Bear right at the top (signposted '**Gribdale**') and walk for a mile or more along an attractive level moorland path with enjoyable views ahead. Keep close to the side of the second plantation and descend steeply, then veer right and cross the road to the gate by the information board.

4 Go up the broad track, which eventually leaves the conifer woodland and crosses heather moorland to **Captain Cook's Monument** on **Easby Moor**, erected in 1827 in memory of 'the celebrated circumnavigator'. Enjoy the fine view, then turn sharp right on a path that goes between two stone gate posts, and then, shortly afterwards at a waymark sign, slants left into

North Yorkshire

woodland and descends steeply. Turn right when a broad forest track is reached, then shortly afterwards turn left to the bottom corner of the wood and into a field.

5 Turn right at the bottom of the field along a bridle path that descends through gorse and keeps by a wall on the right. **Roseberry Topping** again comes impressively into view. The path goes into a sunken lane and continues to descend (in muddy conditions, note that it is firm in the middle). Shortly after a house on the left, turn left down a lane by a 'Weak Bridge' sign. Keep straight on, cross the offending bridge over the railway and continue down the lane. Go round to the right of **Brookside Farm** and down the road. Turn right at the road junction, then go along the enclosed footpath immediately after the first house on the left. Cross the footbridge over the river, keep by the fence on the right, then go across the field to the far right corner. The path cuts across the corner of the next field, then keeps close to a hedge as it goes past sports pitches, straight as a die to **Great Ayton**. Just before the bridge over the river, connoisseurs of such artefacts may note the Victorian urinal, moved from Station Road in 1998. Turn right after the bridge, and the **Royal Oak** is round the corner.

Places of interest nearby

This whole area is full of Captain Cook associations. He was born in 1728 at nearby Marton now part of Middlesbrough, and the family moved to Great Ayton in 1736. A few years later James Cook was apprenticed to a grocer and haberdasher at the North Yorkshire port of Staithes. The **Captain Cook Schoolroom Museum** is on the High Street close to the Royal Oak. You can sit next to him during a lesson, or stand beside him on board ship! ☎ 01642 724296.

9 **Grosmont**

The Station Tavern

This walk explores the beautiful steep-sided valley of the Murk Esk that runs down from the North York Moors near Goathland. Starting at Grosmont, you will follow a route along the side of the valley through woodland, pasture and moorland. The return to Grosmont is downhill all the way, much of the time along the attractive route of an old, once horse-drawn, tramway. As well as appealing to lovers of fine scenery, the walk caters for railway buffs, who not only have the tramway to savour, but sounds and glimpses of steam trains on the nearby North Yorkshire Moors Railway. Devotees of the TV serial *Heartbeat* will also appreciate the walk, as Aidenfield is a pseudonym for Goathland. Those who do not want to do the whole circuit can go as far as Goathland and return to Grosmont by train, or even easier take the train to Goathland and walk back. Another option is to do a shorter circular walk via Beck Hole. Grosmont is a former industrial village and one can still see the remains of blast furnaces, which used ore mined locally.

THE PUB

The **Station Tavern** at Grosmont was built in 1836. On a warm day, you can have a meal and quaff your beer outside and watch the steam trains go over the nearby level crossing. There is a good selection of food (which is served on big platters) and dishes include fresh Whitby cod and home-cooked chicken and ham pie. The real ales are Greene King, Camerons Strongarm and John Smith's. Bed and breakfast is also available here.

The pub is open all day and serves food from 12 noon to 2.30 pm and 7 pm to 8.45 pm.
☎ *01947 895060*

Distance – Full circuit 7½ miles, Beck Hole circuit 5 miles, linear walk to Goathland just under 4 miles.

OS Explorer Outdoor Leisure 27 North York Moors: Eastern area. GR 828052.

Starting point The Station Tavern at Grosmont.

How to get there *Grosmont is 6 miles south-west of Whitby. Take the A169 Pickering to Whitby road, and 15 miles from Pickering, turn off westwards to Grosmont down a minor road with a steep descent. The Station Tavern is on the right just before the level crossing. Grosmont can be reached by rail from Pickering (North Yorkshire Moors Railway) or via the Middlesbrough-Whitby line.*

POCKET
PUB WALKS

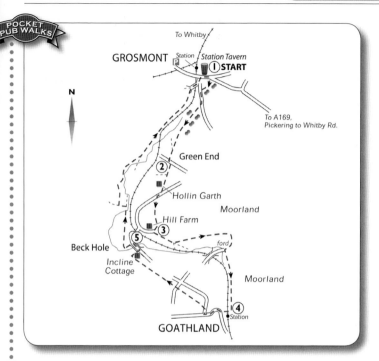

To Whitby

GROSMONT *Station* / *Station Tavern*
P   ① **START**

N

To A169,
Pickering to Whitby Rd.

Green End

②

Hollin Garth

Moorland

Hill Farm

③

⑤   ford

Beck Hole

Incline
Cottage

Moorland

④
Station

GOATHLAND

---

1 Leave the pub and turn left up the steep street. Look out for a well-concealed footpath sign on the right after a few hundred yards (if you get to the road junction you've gone too far). The path descends into a wood and crosses a footbridge. Turn left along a tarmac lane, go through a gate and shortly afterwards bear right at a footpath sign along a paved path. The path enters **Crag Cliff Wood**, climbing steadily. Toots and whistles from the engine sheds in the valley below mingle with the birdsong. Cross a footbridge and continue along two fields before re-entering woodland. Almost immediately, go over a stile on the left and along the top of a field and into further woodland (with muddy sections). Turn left into a green lane soon after leaving the wood, go through two stone gateposts (avoiding the gate on the right)

49

towards the hamlet of **Green End**, then to the left of a low, pantiled barn.

2 Turn left up the road, then soon turn right by a footpath sign. Go through a farmyard and continue along the farm track with a hedge on the right. Keep straight on when the track turns right and go to the left of the farm at **Hollin Garth**. Turn right when the road is reached, then at a footpath sign after a few yards turn left along a level moorland path, soon joined by a wall on the right. Turn right at a junction of paths and walk down to **Hill Farm**.

For the shorter circuit, continue down the tarmac road past the farm, go left at the road junction by the railway bridge and walk down into **Beck Hole**, then follow the route described in point 5.

3 *For the longer circuit,* turn left by the footpath sign at **Hill Farm**, and continue along the path at the bottom of the moor to an attractively sited seat overlooking the valley (also a good place to watch the trains). To view the nearby **Thomason Foss waterfall** choose the right-hand path of the three on offer, but take great care. To continue the walk, take the left-hand path that steadily climbs the moor with good views down into the valley (this is a de facto path on access land). After a gate go to the left of a house and straight on to a stile, then turn right and descend steeply. Turn right after the footbridge, then, just before the ford and stepping stones over the **Eller Beck**, turn left along a grassy path that soon climbs steeply up the left side of the wooded railway cutting before dropping down to **Goathland Station**.

4 Cross the line and continue up the road into **Goathland**. Just after the **Goathland Hotel**, turn right on the road to **Darnholme**, go past the car park and toilets, then turn left on the path marked '**Grosmont Rail Trail**'. You are now on the old tramway. Keep along it for almost a mile, descending quite steeply. Just after **Incline Cottage** (a pleasant bit of early railway architecture), turn right at a crossroads of paths on the bridleway to **Beck**

Hole. Turn left when the road is reached, past the pub and across the bridge over the river – a most attractive spot.

5 Immediately after a cottage called **White House**, turn left, through a gate and along a path that soon leads back to the tramway (*those doing the shorter walk*: turn right immediately before White House). Turn right, and continue along the tramway, though first pause to read the various plaques about the history of the line. Built by George Stephenson as a horse-drawn tramway, it opened in 1836 and was later improved to take steam engines before being closed in 1865.

Continue along the tramway and ignore the **Rail Trail**, which turns off on the right. Shortly afterwards, turn left on a broad track to a gate marked '**Egton**', then turn right and go over a footbridge on a path signposted to **Grosmont**. The clear, but little-used path keeps to the bottom of rough meadowland, never far from the river. After ½ mile it rejoins the tramway at a stile by a gate. Turn left along the tramway and keep going. The path goes to the other side of the fence when the **North Yorkshire Moors Railway engine sheds** are reached, and climbs up a short hill from which there is a good view of **Grosmont**. Turn right at the seat (the railway is below in a tunnel), left on the **Rail Trail** past the church, then come out into the village opposite the pub.

Places of interest nearby

The **North Yorkshire Moors Railway** is an 18-mile line from Grosmont to Pickering, and takes a scenic route through moors and dales. There are several daily trains throughout the summer months, many of them pulled by steam engines. Some of the trains now go through to Whitby.
☎ *01751 472508*

The Victoria Hotel

If you enjoy sea views, you will love this walk, as Robin Hood's Bay is in sight virtually all of the time. The route starts close to Boggle Hole, a cleft in the cliffs, and climbs up the hillside at the back of the bay. It then descends towards the sea, and returns by the Cleveland Way along the edge of the cliffs (there are no vertiginous moments). The walk also visits the site of the former Peak Alum Works, now a place of beauty belonging to the National Trust. This is an excellent route for wild flowers, and orchids will be found on the banks and cliffs in late spring and summer.

For the energetic who do not mind adding 1½ miles each way, the walk can be commenced from Robin Hood's Bay (the village), where there is a car park close to the Victoria Hotel, and another car park further up on the site of the former railway station. From there, simply walk down almost to the shore, then turn right along the Cleveland Way to Boggle Hole, then up the steep lane to the car park at point 1.

THE PUB

The **Victoria Hotel** is on the left of the main road into Robin Hood's Bay (B1447), just before the steep drop into the old village (known locally as simply 'Bay'). It is a privately owned and run pub, which also does accommodation (10 en suite rooms). A wide-ranging menu is served in the bar and also in the dining room at weekends. The haddock and chips and the home-made steak pie are very popular. The real ales are Camerons and Banks, plus two guest beers.

Food is available from 12 noon till 2 pm and 6.30 pm to 9 pm.
☎ *01947 880205*

Distance – 5 miles (or 8 miles if you start in the village of Robin Hood's Bay).

OS Explorer Outdoor Leisure 27 North York Moors: Eastern area. GR 952037.

Starting point The roadside car park above Boggle Hole.

How to get there *Leave the A171 Scarborough to Whitby road 12 miles from Scarborough, and go down the lane to Boggle Hole to reach the car park on the right after 2½ miles.*

North Yorkshire

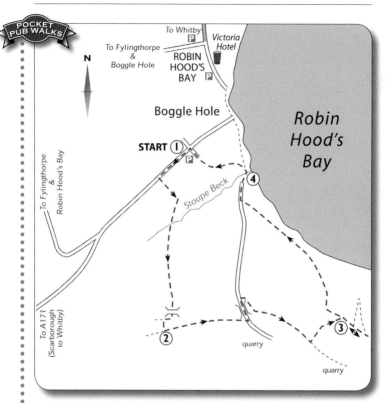

POCKET
PUB WALKS

To Whitby
Victoria Hotel

To Fylingthorpe & Boggle Hole

ROBIN HOOD'S BAY

N

Boggle Hole

START

Stoupe Beck

Robin Hood's Bay

To Fylingthorpe & Robin Hood's Bay

To A171 (Scarborough to Whitby)

2

4

3

quarry

quarry

[1] From the car park at **Boggle Hole** walk up the road away from the sea for 300 yards, then go over a ladder stile on the left on a path signposted to **Browside**. Keep close to the hedge on the right to the end of the field, then go over a stile (well concealed) and slant down the field. Cross the stream by a footbridge at a curious tilting angle, then climb up the field past a gate on the left to a gate at the top left corner. Go straight up the next field to a stile by a gate at the top (fine views if you glance back), then keep by the hedge on the left in the field after this. Go under the bridge of the former **Scarborough to Whitby railway line**,

Robin Hood's Bay Walk 10

then turn right, keeping the farmhouse on the left. Turn left after the gate and take the lane that climbs steeply up the hillside.

2 Turn left when another lane is reached, and continue along it, climbing gently past scattered housing. There are fine sea views. Turn left when the lane reaches a narrow tarmac road (note the old alum quarry on the right) and descend steeply for a short distance. Immediately after going over the former railway bridge, turn right, and then left along the track of the line as it climbs towards **Ravenscar**. Steam engines must have puffed as heavily up the fairly steep gradient as the walkers and cyclists that now replace them. The banks are full of wild flowers and the views terrific. After ½ mile look out for a stile on the left marked '**Conservation Walks**' (if you reach a quarry on your right, you have gone too far). Go down the steep path: the line is roughly between the two buildings ahead.

3 Turn right when an enclosed path (the **Cleveland Way**) is reached, and continue along it for ¼ mile. Just after the access road to the house, turn left down the attractive path to the former **Peak Alum Works**. Read the notice at the entrance to

Robin Hood's Bay.

the site about the adders. The notice continues: 'Please observe these beautiful creatures from a distance and do not approach or touch.' I have recently been on two warm afternoons and not seen any, but make plenty of noise with your feet and be careful what you touch and where you sit.

Retrace your steps (or use the access road by the house) and turn right along the **Cleveland Way**. Bear right at the gate (there is a signpost) and follow the clear path along the edge of the cliffs with fine views northwards along the bay. Turn right when a road is reached. Go by the right-hand side of the car park when the road ends, and descend steeply to the shore.

4 Cross the footbridge over the **Stoupe Beck** (though you may wish to linger first), and take the left-hand path, which climbs steeply up the hillside. When the path levels out, swing left along a narrow meadow, which leads into a green lane and soon to the car park.

If you started from Robin Hood's Bay, take the right-hand path after the footbridge, and continue along the **Cleveland Way** to **Boggle Hole** and **Robin Hood's Bay village**.

To reach the pub from the car park at point 1, go back towards the A171 for ½ mile, turn right on the narrow, steep and twisting lane to **Fyling Hall**, then right to **Fylingthorpe** and straight on to **Robin Hood's Bay**. Turn right at the T-junction in Robin Hood's Bay and the **Victoria Hotel** is a few yards down the road.

Places of interest nearby

Whitby, 5 miles away, is famous for its picturesque harbour, and abbey on a cliff overlooking the sea. But **Robin Hood's Bay** is one of the most attractive seaside villages in Britain, and you can't do better than wander round its narrow streets (almost entirely pedestrianised), and, if the time is right, watch the tide come in.

11 Forge Valley

Ye Olde Forge Valley Inn

This is an attractive walk on the edge of Scarborough. Much of the route is in the extensive mixed woodlands of Raincliffe Woods, but there is also meadow and waterside walking. There are some good views, including glimpses of the sea. The Forge Valley is a local beauty spot. It takes its name from 14th-century iron forges, which used charcoal from the nearby woods. The woodland is now a nature reserve, and there is even a chance (albeit a very unlikely one) of seeing otters. This is a fairly dry route and a particularly good choice in November when the autumn leaves are at their best.

THE PUB

Ye Olde Forge Valley Inn is in West Ayton on the A170, just west of the bridge over the River Derwent that divides East Ayton and West Ayton. It is an old coaching inn dating

Distance – 5 miles.

OS Explorer Outdoor Leisure 27 North York Moors: Eastern area. GR 984875.

Starting point One of the two small car parks in the Forge Valley close to the road junction at the turning signposted to 'Raincliffe Woods, Lady Edith's Drive'.

How to get there Go to East Ayton, 4 miles from Scarborough on the A170 to Pickering. In the middle of the village, take the road signposted to 'Forge Valley, Hackness'. The car parks are 2 miles along the road.

back to 1758 and still offers overnight accommodation. The pub retains much of its original atmosphere, having resisted the fashion of knocking all of the rooms into one, and is popular with locals and visitors. It has an extensive menu and a specials board. Try the fisherman's pie, or the aubergine moussaka. The real ales are Black Sheep, Caledonian Deuchars and Tetley's.

The pub is open all day, with food served from 12 noon to 2 pm and 6 pm to 8 pm (not Sunday nights and Mondays).
☎ *01723 862146*

1 After the car park, walk along the road towards **Hackness** for ½ mile. Immediately after **Mowthorpe Cottage** turn right on a path signposted to **Scalby**. The grassy path runs along the bank of the **Sea Cut** and there are good views of **Raincliffe Woods** on the right, and of the hillside of **Scalby Nab** on the left. The Sea Cut is used for flood control and takes some of the water from the River Derwent straight to the sea; that which misses the cut continues down the river for another 40 miles.

After less than ½ mile, drop down the bank to the right and go over a stile and footbridge (it's easy to miss: it's where the hedge joins up with the bank). Slant across the corner of the field to a farm track that runs to the right of a plantation. Turn left through a gate at the junction of tracks, then continue along the track on the left side of two short fields. Turn right immediately before the end of the second field to a gate leading into **Raincliffe Woods**.

2 Turn right for a short distance when the road is reached, then go left up the wooded hillside on a path signposted 'public bridleway'. The path goes straight up the hillside, though not too steeply, to meet a wide crushed-stone track. Turn left along the track, which goes more or less level along the hillside, and go right when it forks. The track crosses a more open section, then soon goes back into woodland. Bear right (past a seat) when it again divides, and there are glimpses of the sea through the trees. Bear right again at the next junction of paths (past a bench) along a path that climbs the hillside quite steeply.

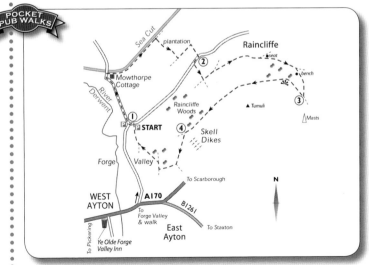

North Yorkshire

3 Turn sharp right when the top is reached (not far from two large masts) along a path that runs just inside the wood with a large open field of **Seamer Moor** on the left. Through the trees on the right there are frequent glimpses of the sea and **Scarborough**, but, frustratingly, never an open view; the best prospect is by a small picnic site where the path bends left. Continue along the path at the side of the wood for over a mile. It is enjoyable level walking and there are some fine Scots pines and beeches. Nearby in the field are tumuli, and the large wooded one in the distance is **Seamer Beacon**.

4 Leave the wood at a gate and go along an enclosed field path with an old stone wall on the left. Just before the gate a tree-covered earthwork called **Skell Dikes** extends across the fields. The path descends gently, and there are good views ahead of the **Yorkshire Wolds**. Turn right when the path re-enters the wood, and shortly afterwards, when the path forks, turn left down the hillside. Almost immediately, there is a splendid view into the **Forge Valley** and further up the **Derwent Valley** to the **North York Moors** (plus an appropriately placed seat). Continue on the path, which slants down the hillside and soon meets the road near the car parks, then drive back down the **Forge Valley** to reach **Ye Olde Forge Valley Inn.**

Places of interest nearby

The **church at Hackness** has much of interest, including, parts of an Anglo-Saxon cross, and some of the building dates back to at least the 11th century.

For those who do not already know it, nearby **Scarborough** is more than worth a visit. You can trace most of England's seaside history in Scarborough, and it has developed on a magnificent site along the bays on either side of its impressive Norman castle.

12 **Rosedale Abbey**

The Milburn Arms

The **North York Moors** are countryside of heather moorlands and steep-sided green valleys. The walk starts at the village of Rosedale Abbey, which is about as deep into the North York Moors as you can get. There are 2 miles of valley walking before a climb to the moors. It is a fairly kindly ascent, but there are a couple of steep bits where conversation will be eclipsed by heavy breathing. Once on the top, there is enjoyable moorland walking along the former railway track and fine views. Additional interest is provided by industrial remains from the days of mining and quarrying in this area, and attempts to locate the abbey.

North Yorkshire

THE PUB The **Milburn Arms**, in the middle of the village, is an attractive pub both inside – where the bar is decorated with photographs of iron mining and the moorland railway – and outside – where a meal or a drink can be enjoyed in warm weather. The pub serves bar meals, and has a restaurant that is open in the evening. There is a separate fish menu, and all the fish is brought fresh every day. Try the smoked salmon, or the baked sea bass grilled with herbs and lemon. The real ales are Marston's, Black Sheep, Taylor's Landlord and Tetley's. The Milburn Arms is residential with a range of en suite rooms.

Food is available from 12 noon to 2 pm and from 6 pm to 9 pm.
☎ *01751 417312*

1 Turn right after leaving the **Milburn Arms**, then right again at the crossroads a few yards further down. Pass the public toilets, then take the road that turns off left. After a short distance go over a stone stile by a green footpath sign (opposite house number 21). Continue along the access road in the caravan park, with the route of the public footpath clearly marked. It leaves the caravan site by a kissing gate next to a metal gate,

Distance – 5 miles.

OS Explorer Outdoor Leisure 26 North York Moors: Western area. GR 725959.

Starting point The Milburn Arms at Rosedale Abbey.

How to get there Leave the A170 at Wrelton, 2 miles from Pickering on the way to Helmsley, and take the minor road up the valley to Welton and Rosedale. Park in Rosedale Abbey village or the car park just above the Milburn Arms.

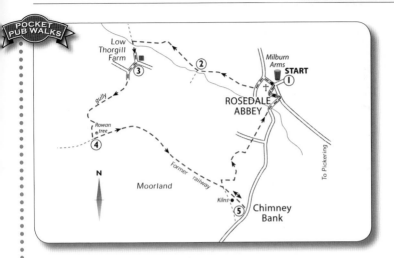

and keeps close to a hedge on the left before descending into the valley bottom.

2 At the junction of paths by the stream (**River Seven**) keep straight on over the duckboards and into meadowland. Immediately after a wooden step stile, turn left down a farm track that leads down to the stream. Go through a farm gate, and follow the fence to a footbridge over the stream (an attractive spot). Go up to a post on the hillside, then to a gate between farm buildings, then straight on through the farmyard of **Low Thorgill Farm** and up a lane.

3 Turn right when the tarmac lane is reached, and when it bends right carry straight on up a lane signed '**Footpath to Farndale**'. Keep to the left of the houses and take a narrow path that goes through a gate on to the moorside. Bear round to the right and keep to the top of a gully as you climb steadily. The path soon comes out at a wall by an isolated rock. Note the several gullies coming down the hillside, and go up the last one you reach (i.e. the far right one). The gully climbs quite steeply and gradually

North Yorkshire

The kilns near Rosedale Abbey.

swings left. Just before it straightens out, take a faint track that goes just to the right of a solitary rowan tree and then becomes a clear path up the hillside to the right of the rounded hillock. Fairly soon, it comes out on the former railway line. The route up the gully to the railway is a de facto path on access territory.

4 Turn left along the former railway. It is enjoyable level walking with typical North Yorkshire moorland on the right, and attractive changing views of the green **Rosedale valley** down below on the left. After a while you reach a convenient decorated seat with the words 'In the dark, working hard, loading up the wooden cart', and on the other side 'Work shift over, in the sun, on the hill having fun'. Continue along the track but when you get to houses on the left and the track swings right, keep straight on along a crushed-stone track. This soon leads to the bottom of a line of stone arches, the kilns of the **Rosedale Iron Works**.

Iron ore mining and quarrying in Rosedale took place between 1856 and 1929, on both sides of the valley. At first the ore went by road to Pickering, then by rail to Whitby. The moorland railway linked up with the main railway network at Battersby

Rosedale Abbey

Junction near Great Ayton, and provided a far better route. To make the ore much more easy and economic to carry in the railway wagons, it was roasted in the kilns to eliminate water and gas.

5 You can now turn left onto the tarmac road and go down the one-in-three **Chimney Bank** into **Rosedale**, and it is a pleasant route with good views. However, for the footpath route, retrace your steps to just beyond the houses, then go down the bank to three ash trees where you will pick up a grassy path. The path turns left at the fence and goes over a wooden step stile. To navigate the mud immediately after, keep as close to the fence as possible. The path descends steeply after this, and it is easy to slip. Go over a stile immediately to the left of the golf course, then over another stile and across the golf course and down to a road. Cross the road, and descend by the fence on the right. The path then goes over a stile, down steep steps in the garden of a house and out onto the road. Turn left, and after a few yards you cross the **River Seven** into **Rosedale Abbey**. Turn left and go round by the church to the **Milburn Arms**.

The 19th-century church was built on the site of the 'abbey', a Cistercian priory which was a community of nuns for four centuries till it failed to survive Henry VIII. There are some fine yews in the churchyard, but few traces of the priory.

Places of interest nearby

Some 4 miles away at the picture-postcard village of Hutton-le-Hole is the three-acre open air **Ryedale Folk Museum** which traces human life in the area from Neolithic times onwards. There are many re-constructed historic buildings, a witch post, and the oldest daylight photographic studio in the country.
☎ *01751 417367*

13 Thixendale

The Cross Keys

The Yorkshire Wolds, many miles of which are in North Yorkshire, surprising though it may seem, are sparsely populated chalk country with steep-sided, often dry, narrow valleys. Some original downland survives on the valley sides. The tops are a land of big fields and wide views. There are three walks on offer: all of them visit attractive Wolds valleys and uplands. The longest route goes to the famous deserted medieval village at Wharram Percy. It is so well worth a visit that if you don't fancy legging it, do a shorter walk, then find your way to Wharram Percy by car.

Distance – 4 miles, 6 miles or 8 miles.

OS Explorer 300 Howardian Hills and Malton. GR 845610.

Starting point The Cross Keys at Thixendale.

How to get there *Thixendale is 18 miles north-east of York. Take the A166 York to Bridlington road, and turn off northwards. If approaching from York, this is the first left after the top of Garrowby Hill. Park in Thixendale village near to the pub.*

THE PUB The **Cross Keys** at Thixendale, attractively situated in a narrow chalkland valley, is a small one-room village pub, and almost entirely unaltered. It is believed to be a former farmhouse and has been a pub since the 19th century. Walkers are very welcome. In winter there are two cheerful real fires and you will always find well-kept real ales (Tetley's and Jennings are the regulars, plus a guest beer). For food, try the home-made steak and Guinness pie, or Lawra's Chestnut Charmer (a chestnut casserole).

Food is served throughout opening times: 12 noon to 3 pm and 6 pm to 11 pm (7 pm to 10.30 pm on Sundays). Bed and breakfast is also available here.
☎ *01377 288272*

[1] Turn right after leaving the pub and shortly afterwards go over the stile by the gate. Keep to the left side of the valley and just above the valley floor. Go over a stile and continue in the same direction to a footpath gate just after a tributary valley on the left (**Court Dale**). The well-signposted path (the **Centenary Way**) turns left up the side of Court Dale (an attractive stretch).

It bears right after a footpath gate, and then turns left, still climbing gently.

2 Shortly afterwards, you come to a junction of paths.

For the 4 mile walk, keep straight on for ¼ mile to point 6, then turn left.

For the longer routes, leave the **Centenary Way**, taking the bridleway on the right. It goes through a belt of young trees then along the top of a field with wide views. Go through the gap in the hedge at the end, then turn right and along the hedge, then left along the side of the field (**Raisthorpe Wold**) with a larch plantation on the right. At the end of the field, go through the gap in the hedge, then turn left along a track with good views

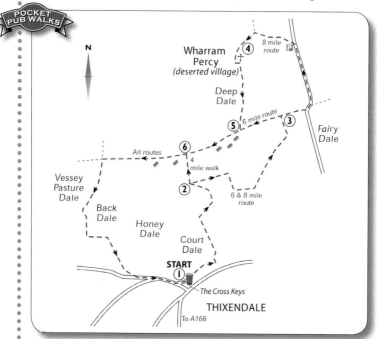

POCKET PUB WALKS

The ruined church in the deserted village of Wharram Percy.

of **Fairy Dale**. After ½ mile of pleasant level walking, the path turns left at a waymark post and goes by a hedge on the left to a junction of paths at the top of the ridge. There is now an extensive view northwards.

3 *For the 6 mile walk,* turn left to point 5 and follow the track south-westwards, as described, to reach point 6.

For the 8 mile walk, turn right along a track that soon leads to a little-used tarmac road. Turn left. There will soon be extensive views northwards to the **North York Moors**, and **Malton** can also be seen. Just before the trees on the left, turn left at a small car park onto the **Wolds Way** path to **Wharram Percy** (there is an information board about the deserted village). Follow a sunken lane into the valley, cross the former railway line from Malton to Driffield, then after the stile, turn left into the site of the former village of **Wharram Percy**. (See Places of Interest Nearby.)

4 The path goes to the right of the cottages in the valley bottom, to the right of the ruined church and left of the pond. It then climbs the side of the valley and follows the fence on the left with attractive views of **Deep Dale** below.

5 Turn right at the junction of paths when the wood is reached, and follow the track as it climbs gently by a hedge on the left.

6 Ignore the path to the left at the beginning of a belt of trees and continue along the track for more than ½ mile. Turn left at a footpath sign, which is easy to miss – it's at the end of a field where the track meets a farm access road. The path, which is both the **Wolds Way** and **Centenary Way** goes through some trees, then follows a hedge on the left before dropping steeply into the attractive **Vessey Pasture Dale**. It goes over a stile at the bottom, turns left to another stile, then climbs steeply out of the dale by a hedge on the right. The path keeps the hedge on the right as it rounds an arable field at the top of the hill, then crosses a stile and goes to the right of a small wood. After a ladder stile, there is a fine view into the **Thixendale valley** below, and the path joins a chalky track that goes down the hillside into **Thixendale village**. Turn left when the road is reached and walk through the village to the **Cross Keys**.

Places of interest nearby

Wharram Percy, 4 miles from Thixendale, is a deserted medieval village dating from the 10th to 12th centuries on a site that has been used since pre-Roman times. It is maintained by English Heritage, and there are several interesting information boards. The site is also a place of considerable beauty.

14 Nunnington

The Royal Oak

This walk explores as rural a stretch of countryside as can be found anywhere in England. Whichever direction takes the eye, there is an endless vista of fields, woods and low hills, and there is scarcely a blot on the landscape. Caulkleys Bank is a wooded limestone ridge, which provides enjoyable walking and fine views. Both circuits take you beside the River Rye and on pleasant green lanes, and you will come across several conveniently placed seats. The longer route includes a path on the edge of the delightful Caulkleys Wood. A visit to Nunnington Hall and gardens, which belong to the National Trust, could easily be combined with this walk.

Distance – 4½ or 5½ miles.

OS Explorer 300 Howardian Hills and Malton. GR 666792.

Starting point The Royal Oak, Nunnington.

How to get there Take the B1257 Malton to Helmsley road, and one mile on the Helmsley side of Hovingham turn off to Nunnington, which is a mile away at the other side of Caulkleys Bank. Park in the village near the church.

THE PUB The **Royal Oak** at Nunnington is an agreeable small pub on the village main street. At the back of the car park is a farm, and mooing noises are ever present. There is an extensive main course menu, with such dishes as steak pie and fisherman's pot. Real ales are Theakston's and Tetley's.

Food is served from 12 noon till 2 pm and 6.30 pm to 9 pm (closed Mondays).
☎ *01439 748271*

1 Turn right on leaving the **Royal Oak** and walk up the main village street. Go through the gate into the churchyard, and round the 13th-century church to a gate stile at the far left corner of the churchyard. Slant left down the field to a lane. Go straight across left to a path beside a wall, then diagonally left across two fields to a road.

Nunnington Hall, a 17th-century manor house, is 100 yards down the road on the right.

Alternatively, it may be preferred to reach **Nunnington Hall** and point 2 by turning left outside the **Royal Oak** and along the village street.

2 Turn right for a few yards, then left along a footpath. Keep fairly close to the bottom of the field and make for a stile to the right of stone gate posts (a fine lime tree is passed). Make for the left-hand corner of the second field, a pleasant spot by a weir on the **River Rye**, then in the next field go towards the immediate right of the left-hand building (this attractive stone building is the former mill and a leat led to it from the weir). Go through the farmyard and keep in the same direction (not down towards the river) on a path past fine beeches at the bottom of a field. Veer slightly right in the next field, then cross a short field beside the river to **Ness Bridge**. Turn right on the road through **West Ness** to a T-junction.

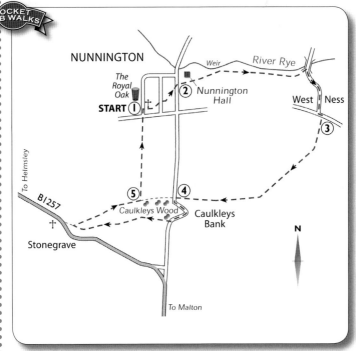

Nunnington Hall is owned by the National Trust.

3 Go left for a few yards, then right on an enclosed track, which soon becomes an attractive green lane (**Caulkleys Lane**). There are increasingly wide views as the lane gradually climbs, and after ⅔ mile it swings right to run along the top of **Caulkleys Bank**, passing a trig point on the right.

4 *For the shorter version of the walk,* when the road is reached, go straight across and continue a short distance along **Caulkleys Bank** to the signpost at point 5.

   For the longer walk, turn left down the road for ¼ mile to a bridleway signposted to **Stonegrave** on the right at the bottom of the hill. The bridleway goes at the bottom of the pleasant mixed woodland of **Caulkleys Wood**. The path eventually leaves the wood and continues close to the fence/hedge at the bottom of a steep field with a view of **Stonegrave church**. At a junction of paths, turn sharp right, and gradually ascend the bank on a delightful grassy path. The path continues through a gate and to the left of the wood, eventually to reach a signpost.

⑤ Turn left (if on the shorter route, turn right) on the track signposted to **Nunnington**. There are good views on the left westwards to **Oswaldkirk** and north-westwards in the direction of **Sutton Bank**. The pleasant track gradually descends to **Nunnington** by the church, and the **Royal Oak** is down the road straight ahead.

Places of interest nearby

Nunnington Hall (National Trust) is a 17th-century manor house with a fine oak-panelled hall and many atmospheric rooms including a haunted one. Its gardens (entirely organically cultivated) are noted for their borders and the orchards of traditional fruit varieties.
☎ *01439 748283*

15 Kilburn

The Forresters Arms Hotel

Kilburn White Horse is one of the great sights of Yorkshire and can be seen from as far away as the outskirts of Leeds. The walk follows well-used paths below the imposing limestone escarpment, which stretches many miles northwards from the White Horse. After Gormire Lake the route climbs the escarpment on an enjoyable wooded path, which is rarely steep. The last part of the circuit goes along the top of Sutton Bank and there are stunning views all the way to the White Horse, as well as precipitous drops close to the feet. These views are an appropriate place to end this book as much of North Yorkshire can be seen. Choose a day when visibility is good to enjoy the walk at its best.

The **Forresters Arms Hotel** is in the middle of Kilburn close to the church, and is an attractive building both inside and out. It dates from the 12th century and retains some of the original atmosphere. There is a specials menu of home-cooked food, which on my visit included Andalusian chicken and fillet of pork with wholegrain mustard, mushroom and cream sauce. In the summer, you can eat or drink outside at the tables in front of the pub. The real ales are John Smith's, Hambleton and Tetley's. There are 10 en suite rooms for overnight accommodation.

Food is available from 12 noon till 2.30 pm and 6.30 pm to 9 pm.
☎ *01347 868386*

1 Turn right after leaving the car park and go down the tree-lined lane. Turn left when a track crosses the road after about 300 yards, and then immediately turn right down a path that keeps just inside the wood and close to the lane. Continue down the

Distance – 6 miles.

OS Explorer Outdoor Leisure 26 North York Moors: Western Area. GR 514812.

Starting point The car park just below the Kilburn White Horse.

How to get there Kilburn lies south of the A170 between Thirsk and Scarborough. Approaching from Thirsk take the A170 and, after 1½ miles, turn right on a minor road signposted to Kilburn, which is reached after a further 4 miles. Just before Kilburn you get a dramatic view of the White Horse on the left. Turn left at the T-junction (signposted 'White Horse') at the beginning of Kilburn, and the car park is on the left after a mile.

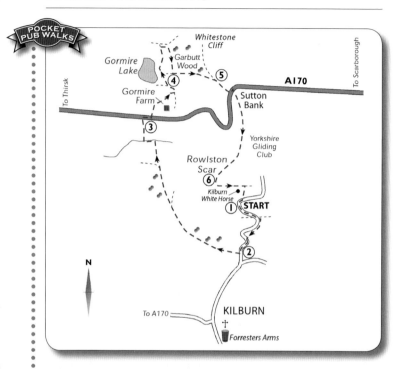

POCKET
PUB WALKS

Whitestone
Cliff

Garbutt
Wood

Gormire
Lake

(4)

(5)

A170

Gormire
Farm

Sutton
Bank

To Thirsk

(3)

Yorkshire
Gliding
Club

Rowlston
Scar

(6)

Kilburn
White Horse

(1) START

To Scarborough

N

To A170

KILBURN

†

Forresters Arms

lane when the path comes out, and then shortly afterwards turn
right when a public bridleway is reached.

2 Go straight on along the bridleway for a mile or more, ignoring
paths and tracks going off at either side. Bear left at the junction
of tracks immediately after a brief descent. From now on there
are fine views to the right of the white limestone cliff that extends
northwards from the **White Horse**. Watch out for a field on the
right, and shortly afterwards look for a signpost on the right
saying '**Bridleway Hood Grange/A170**'. Go along the bridleway,
which is briefly in woodland and then crosses the field. There are
views from the field both to the limestone edge on the right, and
to the **Pennines** across the **Vale of York** to the left. Go left beside

the stream at the end of the field, then over a footbridge and up to the farm road. Go over the ladder stile straight ahead, keep by the fence on the left, then continue in the same direction up the next field to a stile just to the right of a high post.

3 Turn right and go along the A170 for 100 yards (wide verges), then go over a stile on the left by a gate. Cross the field in the direction of the low hill ahead, then shortly after the corner of the hedge, go over a step stile on the right. Slant across the field to a gate on the left (waymark), which leads into an enclosed track. When **Gormire Farm** is reached, keep the farm on the right, then turn right between buildings to a gate. Turn left onto a green lane that soon leads to a gate and signpost.

4 Turn right along the bridleway marked '**Southwoods**', and soon the path goes beside the attractive tree-lined **Gormire Lake**. The path can be muddy (it isn't called Gormire for nothing!). Continue in the same direction and ignore the permissive path on the right (though this can be used for a shorter route). After ⅓ mile, and just before a sign saying 'Thirlby Bank', turn sharp right along a wooded path that climbs steadily. Soon, go over a stile into **Garbutt Wood** on a path signposted 'Sloping Path'. The path keeps more or less level through delightful woodland, passing numbered observation posts. Turn left at the signpost where the permissive path from **Gormire Lake** joins and the path now begins to climb the cliff by an attractive

The Kilburn White Horse.

sloping route. There are a few steep sections, some level stretches and several outstanding views. It would be difficult to imagine a more enjoyable climb.

5 When the top is reached, turn right (signposted '**Cleveland Way, Sutton Bank**'), though some may first wish to make use of the convenient seat. The path goes southwards along the top of **Sutton Bank**, and there is a telescope for those who want more detail. Turn left briefly at **Sutton Bank Top**, then cross the A170 to a signpost, saying '**Cleveland Way, White Horse 1 mile**'. This final mile is exhilarating walking on a well-used path along the limestone edge with immense views across the **Vale of York**. On the left is the **Yorkshire Gliding Club**. The best view of all is from the very end of the edge, where you enjoy the prospect – from the **Wolds** in the south-east, then across the Vale of York and round to the **Pennines**.

6 Follow the path at the top of the **White Horse**. Made of chipped chalk and whitewash, this was constructed in 1857 by a local schoolmaster and his class (what a way to keep them busy!) and was last restored in 2005. Drop down steeply to the car park, the finish of a fine walk.

Return to **Kilburn**, and the **Forresters Arms** is on the left in the middle of the village by the church.

Places of interest nearby

Coxwold, 2 miles from Kilburn, is a village of great charm and is noted for its association with Laurence Sterne, author of *Tristram Shandy*. Sterne was the vicar of Coxwold for several years and lived at Shandy Hall at the top end of the village. Shandy Hall is now a museum and is open to the public on certain days of the year.
☎ *01347 868465*